Lerner SPORTS

...ESPORTS...
TECHNOLOGY

Heather E. Schwartz

Lerner Publications ◆ Minneapolis

T0018735

SPORTS THRILLS
MEET
RESEARCH SKILLS

Lerner SPORTS

Free Database Trial: **lernersports.com**

Lerner Publications Company
An imprint of Lerner Publishing Group, Inc.
241 First Avenue North
Minneapolis, MN 55401 USA

For reading levels and more information, look up this title at www.lernerbooks.com.

Main body text set in Aptifer Sans LT Pro. Typeface provided by Linotype AG.

Designer: Viet Chu
Lerner team: Martha Kranes

Library of Congress Cataloging-in-Publication Data

Names: Schwartz, Heather E. author.
Title: Esports technology / Heather E. Schwartz.
Description: Minneapolis, MN : Lerner Publications , [2024] | Series: Lerner sports. Esports zone | Includes bibliographical references and index. | Audience: Ages 7–11 | Audience: Grades 4–6 | Summary: "New technology is changing the way people watch and play esports. Learn about the technology that makes these competitions possible and what the future holds for esports"— Provided by publisher.
Identifiers: LCCN 2022049972 (print) | LCCN 2022049973 (ebook) | ISBN 9781728490908 (library binding) | ISBN 9798765602935 (paperback) | ISBN 9781728497501 (ebook)
Subjects: LCSH: eSports (Contests)—Juvenile literature. | Video games—Design—Juvenile literature. | Games and technology—Juvenile literature. | BISAC: JUVENILE NONFICTION / Technology / Electricity & Electronics
Classification: LCC GV1469.34.E86 S354 2024 (print) | LCC GV1469.34.E86 (ebook) | DDC 794.8—dc23/eng/20221031

LC record available at https://lccn.loc.gov/2022049972
LC ebook record available at https://lccn.loc.gov/2022049973

Manufactured in the United States of America
1-53021-51039-2/23/2023

TABLE OF CONTENTS

INTRODUCTION
ESPORTS . . . ON MARS?!

The players inched forward, exploring the surface of Mars with an eye out for enemies. They listened carefully for their opponents. It all looked and sounded like a real martian landscape.

Of course, the players weren't really on Mars. They were in a building in Paris, France. The building was transformed by the virtual reality (VR) headsets the players were wearing. The VR made the game seem so real that it was almost impossible for the players to believe they weren't really on Mars.

Esports are video games played in amateur and pro competitions. Like other sports, players compete alone or on a team to win. But esports rely on computer technology instead of sports equipment. New technologies are constantly making esports more exciting and realistic than ever.

Fast Facts

- The first VR Challenger League was held in 2017.

- In 1997, the computer Deep Blue beat world chess champion Garry Kasparov.

- Cloud gaming was worth $1.5 billion worldwide in 2021.

- The esports industry made almost $1.4 billion in the United States in 2022.

CHAPTER 1
CUTTING-EDGE GAMING

HAVE YOU EVER USED YOUR PHONE TO FIND A CREATURE THAT ISN'T ACTUALLY THERE? Games such as *Pokémon GO* bring creatures from games and stories into the real world using augmented reality (AR).

In the 1990s, students at the University of South Australia created an AR mod for the game *Quake*. A mod is a change players make to a video game. This mod was called *ARQuake*. It was the first AR game. Players walked around wearing large headsets and other heavy computer equipment. They fought monsters that appeared around them.

Modern VR headsets are smaller than headsets people wore in the 1990s.

In 2016, Japan hosted its first HADO esports tournament. It was an AR event where players jumped, ran, and battled their way through virtual dodgeball games. Each HADO player wore a small motion detector on their wrist and a few AR trackers. The technology was both light and easy to move around in. It's a big improvement over the very first AR game.

Players in Fuzhou, China, use controllers to track their arm motions as they row boats in a digital game.

When people use VR headsets, they can lose track of their real-world surroundings.

However, AR only adds to reality. VR allows you to enter a completely new world. In virtual reality, the sights and sounds trick your brain into thinking that what you're seeing is real. The real world around you seems to disappear!

Players wearing VR headsets roam inside a large, empty space as they compete inside a virtual battle arena.

VR was invented in the 1960s. Back then, headsets were heavy and attached to the ceiling. It was difficult to move around much. Over decades, the technology became easier to wear. And it works better too!

In 2017, Intel and Oculus announced the first VR Challenger League. Players wore headsets and used controllers to move their virtual bodies. They competed in two VR games for $200,000 in prizes.

Of course, AR and VR wouldn't be nearly as much fun without someone to play against. Some games feature bots or non-player characters (NPCs). Artificial intelligence (AI) controls them. Bots stand in as opponents when there aren't other people to play with. Sometimes players fight against NPCs. But these AI characters often help players on their journeys too.

Gamers play against bots and friends in person and online.

In 1951, the Science Exhibition at the Festival of Britain showcased a computer that allowed players to play the game *Nim*.

World chess champion Garry Kasparov (*right*) plays against the computer IBM Deep Blue.

People have been playing games with NPCs and bots for a long time. In 1952, a game called *Nim* matched people against a machine in a math strategy puzzle. In 1997, the computer IBM Deep Blue beat the world chess champion. It was the first time a computer beat a human in chess history. By 2018, AI had entered the esports arena. AI plays against many of the world's best pro human players.

Z Event was a large gaming event that took place in 2022. Gamers streamed their games and raised money for charity.

But technology doesn't just make esports fun to play. It also makes competitions easier to watch, no matter where you are in the world. Streaming allows you to watch videos on your computer. It started in the 1990s with Internet Protocol Television (IPTV). IPTV was a new way to send video content to viewers through the internet. IPTV was the base for modern technology that allows users to create content and send it out over the internet.

In modern esports, streaming is everything. The first esports event, a *Spacewar!* championship tournament, happened in 1972. About twenty-four players gathered in

TWITCH

In 2011, three million people used the streaming platform Twitch each month. That number grew to 140 million in 2022. Through streaming, Twitch allows everyone with an internet connection to take part in the world of esports. It's the biggest online platform focused on esports.

a computer lab to compete and watch. In later years, large esports events began to draw millions of online viewers from around the world through streaming.

Viewers can watch their favorite streamer and the game they're playing on-screen in real time.

CHAPTER 2
NEW ESPORTS TECH

WITH NEW TECHNOLOGY, ESPORTS ORGANIZERS FIND
NEW WAYS TO PLAY AND WATCH VIDEO GAMES. Some event
planners are putting AR into broadcasts. In 2017, people
watching the ELEAGUE *Injustice 2* event were surprised to
see a virtual Superman smash through the ceiling as he left
the stage.

AR glasses can be light and slim, just like regular glasses.

Tech advances mean live audiences can experience AR too. At an esports championship final in China in 2020, fans received AR glasses. The glasses allowed them to see a virtual dragon flying right in front of them!

POKÉMON GO, THEN AND NOW

On April Fool's Day in 2014, Google announced a fake game in which players could hunt for Pokémon on Google Maps. Two years later, Nintendo and Niantic released the game *Pokémon GO*. In 2021, *Pokémon GO* creators announced the game would become an esport with the 2022 Pokémon Championship Series.

In 2019, *Pokémon GO* players attended an event at Rinko Park in Japan. They caught Pokémon using their phones.

AR only requires a computer or phone screen. But VR requires special equipment, such as a headset, to make the player really feel as if they are in the game. Some games use eye trackers to follow players' eye movements. Wired gloves can help track the motions of a player's hands inside the game. A special treadmill lets players move in any direction in the game without needing a big space to walk around in.

A player uses a special treadmill to move around while playing a VR game.

This equipment isn't cheap, and it's always changing with new technology. Top esports players need the latest gear to stay competitive in VR gaming.

VR players also have to develop physical skills. For example, the game *Echo Arena* is active and fast-paced. Players jump up and crouch down. They grab, punch, and dodge opponents. There's only one way to make those movements happen in the game. The player has to make the movements in real life.

These gamers are playing a racing game. When they move their hands in real life, a motion detector on their wrists lets them control the steering wheel in the game.

In China, people at mental health testing stations are using VR digital therapy to help with stress.

BONUS BENEFITS

Some VR games can help people with mental wellness. Gaming champion Julian Appelanas struggled with social anxiety. Playing VR games gave him a way to talk to people without leaving home. Over time, he grew more confident and less anxious.

A gamer uses an AI program that provides tips
and tricks to get better at a game.

Esports is also a mental game. Some players improve by
using AI programs to coach them. AI programs can learn
human languages. They can also collect player info and
create strategies to beat human players.

AI developers first make sure the AI knows how to
play specific games at a high level. Then the AI program
tracks the player's info and offers strategies to help them

perform better. AI can tell players how to play differently so they'll increase their chances of winning. Pro players are willing to pay for AI training tools that can help them win big prizes.

Winning a match at an esports event can be a big thrill for gamers.

CHAPTER 3
THE FUTURE OF ESPORTS

FOR MANY PEOPLE, A HIGH-END GAMING COMPUTER COSTS TOO MUCH TO EVEN START COMPETING IN ESPORTS. Cloud gaming might change that. In cloud gaming, games are stored and played on remote servers. Servers are computers used to store information, such as games. Players only need a good internet connection to stream games from these servers onto their computers. That helps devices run better.

GET INTO CLOUD GAMING

Cloud gaming isn't completely free. Some gamers pay monthly fees for access to online games. Others pay for game upgrades through small payments. Gamers also pay for games by watching ads. Cloud gaming is a big business. It was worth $1.5 billion worldwide in 2021.

Casual players don't need the best equipment. Gaming systems such as the PlayStation 5 and Xbox Series X already use cloud gaming. Soon, esports may begin using cloud computing as well.

Anybody with a computer and a good internet connection can stream games from the cloud.

Gaming technology is always improving. But much of it used to be thought impossible. In 1992, author Neal Stephenson coined the term *metaverse* in his science fiction novel *Snow Crash*. He imagined a world within computers, similar to VR and AR. Back then, nothing like that existed in real life.

Some people say the metaverse will allow people to meet in virtual spaces using avatars.

Technology is helping people across the world connect through games and digital spaces.

But the metaverse is becoming real. Some say the metaverse is real already. We have digital spaces on the internet where people interact. Others say it's still evolving. They say a true metaverse would include the entire internet and connect the whole digital world.

A gamer wears a full-body VR gaming Teslasuit at the 2019 Consumer Electronics Show in Las Vegas, Nevada.

A metaverse could mean big changes for gaming. Players might wear suits in a real-life arena to control their avatars in battle. On-screen, the fight will play out in a place like ancient Rome. It all looks and feels real—but no one gets hurt.

Metaverse gaming could make games even more exciting for viewers. They could get into the game space virtually, move around, and watch from different angles.

Technology such as VR, AR, and AI used to exist only in science fiction. But gamers and game developers are using them to bring gaming and esports to life. With new tech developments moving forward every day, the world of esports can only get more exciting.

New technology has brought VR gaming to many households.

GLOSSARY

AMATEUR: playing a sport without being paid

AUGMENTED REALITY (AR): an enhanced version of reality created by technology to add digital information onto an image being viewed through a device such as a smartphone camera

AVATAR: an image that represents a computer user in a game

CLOUD: a remote server for storing and accessing data over the internet

MOD: short for *modification*, a change created by players to a video game

PRO: short for *professional*, taking part in an activity to make money

SCIENCE FICTION: made-up stories about the influence of science on society or people

STREAM: to transmit, watch, or listen to online content

VIRTUAL: being on or simulated on a computer or computer network

LEARN MORE

Easy Science for Kids: Video Games
https://easyscienceforkids.com/video-games/

Electronic Sports Facts for Kids
https://kids.kiddle.co/Electronic_sports

Schwartz, Heather E. *Esports Championships*. Minneapolis: Lerner Publications, 2024.

Smibert, Angie. *Video Games from Then to Now*. Mankato, MN: Amicus, 2020.

Szymanski, Jennifer. *Code This!: Puzzles, Games, Challenges, and Computer Coding Concepts for the Problem Solver in You*. Washington, DC: National Geographic, 2019.

INDEX

PHOTO ACKNOWLEDGMENTS

Image credits: OLI SCARFF/AFP/Getty Images, p. 4; Matthew Corley/Shutterstock, p. 6; Flashpop/Getty Images, p. 7; CFOTO/Future Publishing/Getty Images, pp. 8, 21 Luis Alvarez/Getty Images, p. 9; LIONEL BONAVENTURE/AFP/Getty Images, p. 10; Westend61/ Getty Images, p. 11; John Pratt/Keystone/Getty Images, p. 12; AP Photo/H. Rumph, Jr., p. 13; PASCAL GUYOT/AFP/Getty Images, p. 14; Scott Wilson/PA Images/Getty Images, p. 15; Chesnot/Getty Images, p. 16; spooh/Getty Images, p. 17; dekitateyo/Shutterstock, p. 18; Ethan Miller/Getty Images, p. 19; Hero Images Inc/Getty Images, p. 20; Marko Geber/Getty Images, pp. 22, 23, 25; Daniel Krason/Shutterstock, p. 24; BY MOVIE/ Shutterstock, p. 26; NicoElNino/Shutterstock, p. 27; David Williams/Bloomberg/Getty Images, p. 28; WHYFRAME/Shutterstock, p. 29.
Cover: CFOTO/Future Publishing/Getty Images; Imgorthand/Getty Images.